MOTHER DESERT

*

MOTHER DESERT

*

POEMS

JO SARZOTTI

GRAYWOLF PRESS

This publication is made possible in part by a grant provided by the Minnesota State
Arts Board, through an appropriation by the Minnesota State Legislature from the
Minnesota general fund and its arts and cultural heritage fund with money from the
vote of the people of Minnesota on November 4, 2008, and a grant from the Wells Fargo
Foundation Minnesota. Significant support has also been provided by the National
Endowment for the Arts; Target; the McKnight Foundation; and other generous
contributions from foundations, corporations, and individuals. To these organizations
and individuals we offer our heartfelt thanks.

Special funding for this title has been provided by the Jerome Foundation.

Acknowledgment is made to the following publications where poems originally appeared:
Alaska Quarterly Review: "I Dream My Father Drives on Ice"
Borderlands: Texas Poetry Review: "Road Trip," "Appaloosa"
Denver Quarterly: "Perseids over Desert Sea," "The Low Road"
la fovea: "Election," "Perfection"
Margie: "Elephant"
North American Review: "Marilyn in Death Valley"
Perihelion: "Fairy Queen," "The Monotonous Sublime"

Published by Graywolf Press
250 Third Avenue North, Suite 600
Minneapolis, Minnesota 55401

www.graywolfpress.org

Published in the United States of America

ISBN 978-1-55597-615-6

2 4 6 8 9 7 5 3 1
First Graywolf Printing, 2012

Library of Congress Control Number: 2012933709

Cover design: Kyle G. Hunter

Cover photo: © Ken Rosenthal / Corbis

CONTENTS

III

INTRODUCTION

"Perseids over Desert Sea," the first poem in Jo Sarzotti's *Mother Desert*, opens on a desertscape/inland seascape littered with "phantom outboards / Churning jellyfish, ghosts of old / Television commercials," "abandoned / Motels, coyote in the rubble," and the realization that such wonders as the helmet of invisibility and the fountain of youth are "all sham, / Made of horse glue & salt." One way to see this scene is as a map, both geographic and psychological—the kind of map that, in a later poem, Sarzotti calls (describing an elephant's skin) "a map of the world grown old in human / Ruin." The response to this vision of human ruin is this sentence with which "Perseids over Desert Sea" closes: "I walk / To where the land ends / & look out." Which is to say, the response is quiet, undramatic, and—what? In that gesture of looking out, are we meant to see hope, or despair, or ambition (the possibility of escape elsewhere), or folly (for having believed in escape, to begin with)?

This complexity resonating from clear expression, combined with a worldliness—a sense not just of having lived in the world, but of having looked at it, felt it, closely—was what drew me repeatedly back to this manuscript; that, and the sheer pleasure of discovering a strange new sensibility declaring itself with an authority that is rare, these days, often suspect—and yet the authority of these poems increasingly persuades with each reading. I think some of this has to do with confidence of expression, as when, in "The Monotonous Sublime," we are told that

> War lies like a psychopath, a gymnasium
> Of sin, deanimalized & precise,
>
> Working clock-like, seconds counted down to nothing—
> Which is why we chose it.

But Sarzotti trusts in nuance, as well. Outright declarations like the one above are balanced by poems like the one that comes immediately after, "In the Civilized World," in which we encounter Iphigenia, soon to be slaughtered by her father Agamemnon, her sacrifice being required in order for the Greeks to have a wind that will carry them to the Trojan War:

> Wrapped in the wet hide of a dead stag,
> She is her own dowry . . .

> She ascends the altar quietly
> (Obedience
> Her pet dog, invisible at her feet)
> Strapped in her father's leather, mouth
> Gagged open & silent.

> All turn away as the knife
> Descends.
>   She is beatific
> (Dies like a slaughtered doe)
>   In her own blood
> Poured into a stone bowl.

There's an unnerving elegance, stillness, and silence to the entire scene—and this has its own authority. And yet, without saying so directly, Sarzotti is speaking to the classical glamorization of what is ultimately a gruesome and (to our contemporary sensibilities, anyway) senseless act, all in the name of war. Placing "The Monotonous Sublime" next to "In the Civilized World" allows Sarzotti to speak, as well, to the timelessness of war, from classical times to today.

    Back to the helmet of invisibility and the fountain of youth. What the two have in common is that they grant escape—from the sight of others and from the fact of mortality. As we learned earlier, these are shams, and the speakers of these poems admit as much. That does nothing, however, in the way of taming a built-in instinct to escape ("If I drive far enough, fast enough, / Something will change."). This tension between recognizing the fact of one's condition (which we may as well call the human condition) and wanting to believe in the possibility of escape from what one knows is inescapable—this tension is at the heart of these poems' authority and is the psychological narrative, as it were, of the book as a whole. By psychological narrative, I mean something like what happens in Browning's dramatic monologues, crossed perhaps by what happens in those of Bidart; in both instances, nothing is resolved—correctly so, because the point is neither solution nor resolution, but something more like penetration through the surface, into a truer but more disturbing understanding. Or, as Sarzotti puts it in "Naked": "I feel less ground. / I know more. / I see through."

The desire to escape is likely one reason why we are brought to so many places in these poems — Krakow, Prague, Geneva, Iceland, Indiana — and why we encounter such various characters as Flaubert, Juliet, Marilyn Monroe, Emil Nolde; it's as if sensibility here is forever restless, as much so with place as with self, and the self's "inability to heal the lesions of experience," as Sarzotti puts it in "Fatal Familial Insomnia," a poem that ends by suggesting that maybe the only way to escape ourselves is through the surreal:

> I descend
> To the depth of my ancestor's final coma.
>
> The voice of an unearthed pillar
> Tells me, *Go to the cathedral & sleep.*

Another means of escape: the kind of faith that, in these poems at least, is consigned to a lost world. Again, though, that doesn't stop the longing to believe in what isn't believable. Hence, when the speaker in "Appaloosa" chooses a horse to ride, she opts for "the spotted roan's pale glow," a choice that seems random until we are told later:

> For the Nez Perce, the spotted horse was
> Totem & transport to the next home,
>
> Battle, world — I stick to these sweaty sides
> Lashed by leather & mane, an exhalation
>
> Of time on an eastern shore, racing.

It's the speaker's interruption of herself, right after the mention of the Nez Perce's belief, that, again, brings both authority and dramatic situation to the poem, as the speaker seems to want to cancel out (or balance?) a lapse toward older beliefs with the immediacy of sweat, leather, mane — the bodily truth of the horse, its mortality (and by implication, that of the speaker as well), versus the belief that makes escape possible.

> It's the difference between covering the body
> Beautifully & being the body,

Mute & sweaty
In the long last heave of homestretch.

So we are told, in "Fairy Queen." Presentation of self, as opposed to the self in its nakedness, over which a very real anxiety constantly hovers:

I am all

Made of glass, & so
Might break
Into shivering fragments.

("All Horses Die")

The achievement of these poems is in their ability to navigate, meditate upon, and enact—all at the same time—that "long last heave of homestretch," and, against the sometimes overwhelming complexity that comes with being human, to forge a momentary stay (in the form of the poems themselves), not by turning away from reality but by choosing to know it, through and through. It is among the ways in which poetry—and art in general—*can* in fact make something happen. I am changed by Sarzotti's poems, my sense of the world is changed—for that, I am grateful. Bewildered, also—"My map is in pieces." How else can the journey of surprise begin? *Mother Desert* is an arresting debut.

Carl Phillips
June 2011

I

PERSEIDS OVER DESERT SEA

Car dusty & shaking
Hands, brown, lined,
Unknown bruises,
I swear
Nights on the inland sea
There are phantom outboards
Churning jellyfish, ghosts of old
Television commercials —
The skin of it fumes
Softly in the dark,
Air drier than paper
Ripples —
Helmet of invisibility, gold
Bowl, cats on thrones,
Fountain of youth — all sham,
Made of horse glue & salt.
Stars streak like loosed gods,
Perseus conquers Medusa, spews
Light & danger
On the outskirts of town
Long-boarded up, abandoned
Motels, coyote in the rubble,
A dirt road winding
Toward sunset. I walk
To where the land ends
& look out.

MARILYN IN DEATH VALLEY

Platinum hair lacquered in waves, her face
A porcelain bowl of rose petals

At the door of a salt house,
She holds her fingers to her lips, sucking,

Praying, wrapped in a man's denim jacket
As if it were ermine.

The Funeral Mountains drift like a mirage,
Horses are buried in a tear marsh,

Slow-coursing minerals shatter posts
Quietly. Voles scavenge rib cages,

Tunnel bones. Palms are charged with explosives.
A drained swimming pool

Means the owner is dead. Let the phone ring.

ELECTION

Jinx is in the air like the smell of laundry.
I speak

Into a yellow receiver, everyone else is talking
As if to themselves.

A wraith turns & curses. This may be the Bardo.
I may not be awake.

You may not be dead.
Perhaps I just got out of jail & you are on the line.

A Spanish girl with red-gold threads in her hair
Pockets her phone,

Spike-heels
To machine elves with metal arms, the poll.

Perhaps I'm the Spanish girl. Perhaps you
(As dog) are late for work.

There is a hell
Nor am I out of it. I vote later.

THE MONOTONOUS SUBLIME

War is a box of silk & dogs tipped, half-buried
In many small horrors.

Paratroopers descend on the maroon of desert.
Dust storms spike an ocean of sand,

Heave & upwell, dip & pool
Scratched & scraped by a patient lithographer,

Everything imagined backward.
The horizon showing is too much brain

Showing, too much edge denuded of guilt.
It is erased, smoked out.

The bridge, too tall & although beautiful, weak,
Falls into a great river

Of god, an ancient crawl of damage, no repose.
The hoof of a sphinx

Remains, an image of waiting.
The bull of heaven crumbles.

War lies like a psychopath, a gymnasium
Of sin, deanimalized & precise,

Working clock-like, seconds counted down to nothing—
Which is why we chose it.

In the Civilized World

Wrapped in the wet hide of a dead stag,
She is her own dowry,
(Men stranded,
Getting darker each day)

Her bridegroom
All the Greek war dead
(Paid in advance,
            For the unborn)
Stalled between land & sea.

She ascends the altar quietly
(Obedience
Her pet dog, invisible at her feet)
Strapped in her father's leather, mouth
Gagged open & silent.

All turn away as the knife
Descends.
        She is beatific
(Dies like a slaughtered doe)
                In her own blood
Poured into a stone bowl.

The wind noosed around her throat
Rises. Flat sails fill
 (Pregnant bellies, a great red birth)
In the cold huddle & worry
Of men.

7

CORDELIA TAKES A POWDER

I wore an overcoat in case there was bad weather
In the world of sex. All I had was one outfit.
I took my purse. He watched television all day,

Stretched deep in a slashed velvet couch,
Tiny spiders snugged in his mute grey beard, breeding.
He swallowed words I needed, leaving only *the*.

I don't believe in a just God.
For example, schizophrenics can't smell. I can't smell.
They have no *here*. I have one *the*.

The words had something in common with romance.
If only there'd been a mother.
If only I could heave my heart into my mouth.

ABANDON/MENT

The trombones are in Rotterdam
To celebrate the king,
Brass parades
In boulevard
& lane.

One left out
Weeps,
Torn shoulder, a beautiful boy
But sickly,
Won't live long—

At home, we wait,
Grow mossy
In a slatted wood
Open to the north,
Shady & damp, far

From the grand
Harbor of a foreign city
Where ship masts spike
Pale sky
Reflected in shining water.

The industry of men
In boats, sails
Dropped
& tied,
Oars dip.

Natural History

She loves the sublime shrunken ghouls under glass,

Eyes laced shut in continuous reverie of locked violence.

The skirt of her colonial white dress floats

From its pinched waist over bare feet gathering splinters

In the word hoard, dusty file for bees tucked in leaves,

Sugar ants streaming from broken spines.

She stacks books on her head like a savage in ancient heather.

Her long hair sweeps the floor.

This is my girl, musket-toting, mummy-hunting.

Blue sky boils painterly clouds caught on gothic spires.

Her heart of darkness a mote I keep in my small eye.

THE YEAR THERE IS NO SUMMER

No first blade, no grain in the ear, come October,
A cornucopia of sand.

In Villa Diodati, genius makes its own weather,
Knowing no season,

Sews monsters together, rescues the buried alive,
Dresses them in tuxedos.

News of foreign wars confirms that life continues.
They sail on

A phosphorus sea to a diamond shore, lie on beds of ore,
Soar into an acid sky

On mechanical wings, a great lifting.

FLAUBERT

In winter, bad news piles on the floor.
Books, desk unopened,

Papers unsorted — I am suffocating.
Discarded light

Gathers in unexpected corners,
My cat, a *doppelganger*,

Suns all afternoon, eyes green & piercing.
I fall in a meadow,

Faint driving a carriage. My brother
Bleeds me by the roadside,

Horses impatient, my mother
A weeping statue.

I long to be a woman, own a slave,
Taste human flesh,

Burst.

PRAGUE

Her fingers numb as a marionette's,
Cold as stained-glass,

Needle prick to skin lifts up a little tent.
The cardboard city unfolds

Like a child's cut-out, angels fly
Through a glass syringe

Into narrow lanes of snow. Heretical
Longing for alchemy in street of gold,

She buys a ceramic pipe, postcards:
Castle with cone roof, Apostle clock.

Distilled, dispelled, she is pierced,
Leveled, lashed & thrown.

Her breath freezes
In whispers of ice, stars blink.

MELANCHOLIA

The old man looks more confused each day.
I sit in my own blue corner,
Skin the color of stable stone,

Hair tangled. My ailing dog grows
Thinner, the cherub on the floor
Scribbles incessantly.

I used to ride in the park every morning,
Saddling my horse
In a stall of manured hay,

Careful in streets, shy of noise. Now
Nobody rides. No more flanks
Of sorrel & bay through trees.

The old man can't find his apartment.
I guide him home,
Offer to walk his dogs. My place is a mess,

Hammer & nails, little blocks of wood
Scattered about like grown up toys
Abandoned.

Outside, the durable sea, the horizon.
Inside, an unstirred cauldron
Waiting for wind from an angel's wing.

EMIL NOLDE

Saturating tiny sheets of Japan,
Thick layers no one can see through,

He is a mountain giant in a closet,
Wind at whim, or opened door.

The agenda is breathtakingly stupid,
An opera of brown sky, red clouds.

Banished, no painting, no sunlight, no models,
Even the air keeps the secret: no odor of oil.

Blue broods solid & solemn, fairy shapes
The hounds cannot see

As he wades through dark purple
Touching green sky, white bird on his chest,

Figures holding children spilling over the edges
Of his unlawful mind.

TURNERESQUE

On the trestle, the train
Keeps coming, black blaze, furnace.

Water & sky struggle to be blue,
A boat, a distant town bombarded by gold.

My northern blood forgets
Sheered pastures under deep snow

Blinded by what city does to country,
Honeycombed dwellings, their spotless interiors

& all the while, putting muddy palm prints
Wherever I can.

Underground, north is a blur
Through scratched & yellowed windows,

School children on the platform
Telescope smaller, smaller,

The train hurtling
Into a tunnel & I to myself,

A mouthful of air.

The Low Road

If the power comes on after a count of five, it means a swan hit the line.

In a pub at the end of the Scottish north, light matters.

Far from long sunsets over the San Andreas Fault & Soda Lake

I have imposed Solitary Confinement with single malt.

Some here remember Odin, god of bad weather,

Philosophy as commonplace as eating coastal cheddar, meat pie.

Sheep fleck landscape, wool & lunch on the hoof.

The suicide rate is low, even among magicians & poets,

Anomie almost unheard of, life is so hard

Like the ground, Bifrost Bridge lifting everyone's spirits.

Mirrored over the bar in amber & brown, fifty-nine reasons to keep drinking.

TATTOO

Deep in the underworld, gods
Know they are dead.
Fettered monsters, never loosed,
Squeeze me between planks
Upholstered with kindness
I cannot tolerate.

Hard in a wolf's jaw, my hand
To the wrist, wolf bone, venom burns
Australia on my forearm.
Boots cobbled of scrap leather,
Ships made of clipped nails,
Nothing saves me.

SOON WINTER

The giant whose breath has burned
The back of my shirt all year is gone
Underground.

The gold of prodigal October spent,
It litters the path with riches
No one wants.

Perhaps I'll lie down with the cows
In their still-green pasture, let them lick
Salt from my face

Like the Norse rime mother's
Warm tongue makes white ice human.
In a land

Always cold, always light
One can see the end coming.
November

Has me deep in dark hollows
Weaving a cloak of feathers, birds
Already flown.

ELEPHANT

God of mud & wallow, it can blight a field,
Comfort the dying,

Destroy a marketplace. Its rage is motherless,
Nurtured by no one,

Fed by chain & dust. It fights for its young,
Mourns its dead, lives on.

Armored for war, its triumphal procession
Is too wide for city gates.

Piles of tusk float on barges to Cairo, harvested
Precious & female from the jungle.

Its sanctuary is manmade, its memory a long night
Of weeping.

Its skin a map of the world grown old in human
Ruin. Its body,

Eye, ear, tail, knee, trunk, a blinded mirror.

II

MINIATURE

My father's dump truck tilts
Earth to the ground,
My mother squints at me, pins
In her mouth.

All the dead pets thrive, the horse
I never learned to ride,
(My grandfather whispering,
"You have to show them who's boss.")

The cat who had six litters,
Relatives with bitter faces,
High school friends
Still young.

Dread flies in the night
Seeking the small & sickly,
Stirs old graves, robs
Their colored glass.

I ride behind,
Tailpipe burning bare leg,
Always wanting to be carried
To a wild other.

KRAKOW

I am skinless, all nerve
In this city of crocodiles
Ground to apothecary dust,
Dragon moat filled with dirt,
'Aus' on a sign glimpsed
From the train, ghosts of tanks,
Too dark too early, December
Lights up for Christmas
Broken ghetto walls
Plastered with rock & roll.
I shiver in the iron
Gaze of mutilated angels,
Town square, snow
Cold & hard under boots,
A hooded beggar in white
Poses for money. I pay him
To sit down. He offers to hold
My tin crèche. I trade it
For his muslin, try on
The ghost I will become.

I Dream My Father Drives on Ice

What the ice says bodies stress & hardness,
Brittle breaking
Like china shattered, door slammed,
Footsteps on flagstone
Leaving—he strains for the sound
Of a pane of glass
On a hard frost night—he knows to worry
When he hears nothing,
Ice road rivering aqua, wild cold, frozen lakes,
Bleached tundra.

Ravens score the sky, dance around upturned ribs
Of slain caribou,
One treads air at his window so close he can see
The black bead in its eye.
In April the ice goes spongy & silent, the road
Collapses.

Seagulls on the beach beg food
From children.
Summer striped umbrellas, white sand
Hot underfoot,
He carries me on his shoulders, tanned forearms,
V at his neck,
Eyes like mine ice blue. We listen to surf
In shells, we know
To worry when we hear nothing.

ANATOMY OF RUIN

The bus stop oasis,
The bus itself an animal humping up out of

Dark matter. I get on & ride home to tell you
Something untrue.

The salt factory sways like a scaffold, detonated
But refusing to fall.

I mistake a spring day for November,
My ruin.

FLYING

No wings lift the horse, a wished-
On dandelion floats, each leap
Lands a descending eagle
Grabbing frightened prey,
Kicks a divot of iron-red turf.

Everything's wrong with my life.

Plato says the soul can grow wings
If swept up in a stream of longing
For beauty.

The next jump rushes,
Touch, launch, terror & bone,
Stir of muscle under sleek-
Haired skin, bumps I imagine
Rising on my shoulders.

FAIL ROAD, INDIANA

An emporium of needs: the mouth
Of my mother's dirt, shells on the beach.

I am part of then.   A long body stopped,
As if there has been a death.

Nothing divides me from a pile of sticks.
Three sorrel draft horses huddled in a sea of milk,

A plank barn, its silo
For all the world a lighthouse on the brink.

I lose an hour.   I drive west.

ROAD TRIP

Sunset, a red magnetic eye,
Darkness, dread,
Headlights—

If I drive far enough, fast enough,
Something will change.

Come morning
The giant eye in mine
Sees beauty is no accident.

Horses pound hours into the road,
My map is in pieces.

A dead animal blots the yellow line,
Natural taxidermy,
Flattened & dried, particalized,

It is the sting in desert wind—
I've left myself.

The dead thing stares back,
Won't retreat, gives no quarter—
I wonder what it was,
A matted fur mandala,
Deliverance? I forget the way back.

But I believe the road will save me.
It sings a lullaby,
Tucks me into green oases,

Shelters me in salt hollows.

WEST, WHERE THINGS END

The young man's limbs & long hair stream
In slow motion toward the water,

A pennant of fog on a spike of orange
Iron. The suspended span swings, a gate

Jumpers slip through,
Their conversation with the bridge ever-

Secret, god knows.

FATAL FAMILIAL INSOMNIA

I stand all night at the mirror combing my hair,
Coarse white shirt, rope belt gone, stripped

Eyes withered like old harvest.
My disease is familial: fatal blistering

& inability to heal the lesions of experience
Murders sleep, exhausts body.

My mother is an oval memory,
White bridal satin, a hundred covered buttons,

She leans against my father's dark sleeve, smiling,
Wary, skinned in light.

An ancient villa stirs, red stairs curl around
To the street, a subway sign

Glows xenon blue. I descend
To the depth of my ancestor's final coma.

The voice of an unearthed pillar
Tells me, *Go to the cathedral & sleep.*

PERFECTION

I eat, don't eat
Which breeds a predator's alertness
Thin as a sheet
Of cigarette paper, harmless
As cream.

Starving
I pick salad from plastic, raisins out of the bun
Refusing (Using)
A tiny metal bowl in the company
Of others.

I am heroine,
Gladiator in lion ring. My mother,
Her cadaverous
(Fallen) hand, grace around a bone cup,
Does not scare me,

Her lips about to touch the skin of milk
Forever parted.

INFINITE SPUR

Only one kind of wind
On this un-fleshed spine,
The best way down
Is to keep climbing
God's beard,
Cloud spilled over the ridge,
Vertical maze, rope
Frozen in ice, pack
Already gone, & radio.
I start making deals,
Flush the last swallow
From under my roof,
Become the breath of a fish,
Noise of a cat's step,
Root of a mountain.

THE SCREEN OF HIS RETIREMENT

Pale, arthritic, eyes failing, he seldom leaves
Warm winter sanctuary under a shedding oak,
Keeps twenty medicines on a tray close at hand,
Chocolate hidden in tufted folds of an old warrior's chair,
Misses the hunt, the chill, the gray kill at dawn,
Ash tree, wolves in the throne room.

The pulse of helicopter blades beats the air flat on his ears.
Sirens announce the arrival of Valkyries in white coats
Leading an eight-legged horse out of the mist,
Chrome sheen, muffle of muslin sheet, his last ride.

FUNERAL DOVE

Waxed & powdered exactitudes:
Ruby maroon flowers, pinecone
Tipped on the sidewalk, your face.

California cloud-ripped sky,
Persimmons on leafless branches,
A muddy colt nobody has time to break.

At the service, I cannot hear myself,
Read my poem in a borrowed voice,
Take communion, though I've not confessed,

Touch your closed coffin. Green winter
Streams limousine windows,
Tattooed hands release a dove at graveside.

You sit on my pony bareback, your feet
Near the ground. I sit in front,
Fingers in wiry mane, holding on.

HALF OF LIFE

Yellow leaves bend into the lake,
Shore massed with vines
Of tangled bittersweet.
Two cormorants glide in circles,
Then disappear under water
So long I look away,
See my father,
Foot poised on a shovel,
Handle between his fists,
Bend & spoon out
A piece of dark red earth.

O, where will I pitch my crying tent
When bare cold winter comes,
The ground impenetrable,
Leafless trees swaying,
Endless icy moan.

ICELAND

Two combs & a cudgel rest on the sill.
Fire blazes a small volcano in the wall.

Bodies move slowly, sounds of waking
Bang in flat, cold morning.

The chart of this land is lost.
When snow lies thick on the heath,

Small flowers cased in deep seed,
Stray sheep huddle near frozen water

Until men on bone skates find them.
Day is short, sky gray.

For horned & hornless creatures
There is no pasture.

AFTER THE DEMOLITION

There is only one picture of you, mouth
A red slash, brow a whole world to die in.

I've stayed here on Red Creek Road, hair
Long & well-tended, skin papery,

Wrists scarred by knotweed & rosehip,
Ladders to climb into a better place.

Traveler to the origin of bleat & gut,
I've forgotten how to eat.

We were a lucky mirror, waiting
For the wrecking ball.

LABOR

Circles of pain body me
Alone with secrets God whispers,
Fiery arrows shot again & again
As if I were his saint,
I scream, *Don't Touch Me!*
Sweat, muscle & gland inexorable,
If I were an animal, I would be me.
Mob of gel & mucous,
Angel in a searing tide—
I would do it again

CAPITAL PUNISHMENT

It's cold, like an operating room,
Hard straps pull me
Toward a deep ravine.
No pillow.

I call the lung man.
I call the police.
I pray for rain.

The moon is an envious old monk
Peeping Tom,
A cat on carpeted stars
Lapping milk.

IN MEDIAS RES

Bodies dig, cough to death,
Babies gurgle & ray like stars,
Forgotten.

Horses graze, the lame one nickers.
I lie deep in green walls
Wishing myself

Burst into oak, long days
Of earth-drawn water,
Branches battling

Over home, wind indifferent
As drugged sleep, nightmare proof,
Proof of pain.

Appaloosa

The dark drift of horses in stalls, black
Windows on still blacker shapes,

The barn is quiet and heavy —
I stop at the spotted roan's pale glow.

He's the one I take out to ride,
Ears pointed like an Egyptian guard dog,

Excited tear toward the beach, white surf
Tattered by wind, sickle moon a gash

In the sky god's thigh, pinpricks of starlight,
The crab nebula, rare gift of August,

Stained glass from a cosmic cathedral
Exploded — the horse shies sideways, neighing.

For the Nez Perce, the spotted horse was
Totem & transport to the next home,

Battle, world — I stick to these sweaty sides
Lashed by leather & mane, an exhalation

Of time on an eastern shore, racing.

ROCK EDICT

If light is the natural agent that makes
All things visible, what causes this cast-

Adrift feeling of loosened hinges,
Unhooked flags? I am ever northern, a poor

Shell of self, never not in ice & sand, I take
Meals of hardtack & clouded water, sleep in a tent,

My rough coat not quite thick enough
To bear winter hail in a brittle desert crossing, or

Resist the yellow-eyed animal at each border.
I pass through saffron gates, up a snow-covered path

Toward a mountain shrine & blue-black sky,
Past a frontier post inscribed, *Be Harmed*.

TAIPEI

Coiled around my own drowning,
I wait in the night market.

Everything here is for sale—bottled snake,
Cooked meat in stiff paper,

Braids of human hair,
The hot breath of children.

I can't speak the language: bells, houses
Cracked by lightning.

My skin pales, creases like white iris.
I will live in the jungle

Under banyan trees with an ocean view.
My life as lioness will begin.

III

NAKED

This deep
Blue space —skeleton
Afloat

In my inland sea,
Clavicle,
Most graceful of bones,

Wing without feathers,
Swan Lake
Leaking into liquid light,

Rib cage,
Pale choir in a cathedral
Of shade,

Held breath
A little death
Caged in glass,

Film, white florescence,
The doctor's arm
Pointing,

I feel less ground.
I know more.
I see through.

Feed Not Things with Sharp Teeth

Wound in my nightgown,
A premature shroud,
I kick dogs of pain,

Conjure the lavender farm,
Rows of color
Around a brown knoll

Squeezed into a hard knot,
Bone lifted to sky,
Bed of lye, aged barley,

Eight withered grapes
Soaked in gin.

The devil rests
Behind the iron stove,

Afraid of light.

THE COMMODORE TAKES A LOVER

Séance on translucent skin, she summons spirits
Whispering forgiveness.

His hand on her belly,
Bedroom, boardroom apparitions disappear,

Her powdered legs
Wrap his mahogany soul in gaudy solace.

In his mouth, she places a sparrow, struck
Dead in mid-flight,

Still warm, wings folded, feathered body
Dissolves.

RITE OF PASSAGE

Day begins in bare laboratory light,
Trash & sweat.
He applies ether-soaked rag,
Then snips each
Rib cage with kitchen shears.
The worst outcome imaginable
Is waking.

Each small death is hell,
Shell after shell
Plugged into the deep hidden heart
Of a great tusked beast
Taking hours to die on a dusty plain,
A horde of villagers
Waiting for a bit of meat.

He prints date & time on neat tags.
When he can't kill anymore,
He comes home.

SLEEPING ON THE BEACH IN TULUM

Even here I think of elephants, fanned ears
Like a Pharaoh's crown,
How a mother uses her trunk to lift
A sick newborn into shade, how few trees
Grow underground.

White lip of surf, your rhythmic small
Lion's roar of breathing—
We've brought an elephant with us,
This afternoon, it pulled up palms,
Slammed a tourist bus, broke a bicycle.

Now it rests at our feet. I call it into the waves.
Spraying water like a serpentine fountain,
Young & small, it shrinks, a baby, then nothing at all.

FALSE FORD

Your spotted roan arrives riderless,
Sinks to his flanks,
Unable to find footing in the deep lynn,
Reins flailing.

I am the river nixie waiting for you
To come across
Where I seem shallow,
But you are asleep at home

On clean sheets & straw,
Full of liquor.
I plunge into a canyon, so fast & steep
Boulders are scrubbed white.

In the morning I return
To my own shape,
Each time
A little smaller.

ALSO CALLED SPHINX

Hawk moth on the screen door
Wide as two hands
Winks into the air, a great
Parted eye lifting over lawn,
Edge of bay eel-grass
Ribbons, bracken curls.
A white spider binds a wasp
In Queen Anne's Lace,
Moored sailboats drift,
Pink streaks the fog
For sunset, then night.
I never hurt
Anyone on purpose,
Not really.

THANATOS

Not the way my mother's chin looked,
Not my father's waxed cheek,
But a room

I could enter even if it had no door
& stand in the still center of panic
At a water hole,

Stampede of hoof & claw, elephants
Holding ground, their young huddled
Against great gray legs,

Like me, for the moment, safe.
Then gone. A faded acuity in the air
All that remains.

Great tree of beaten gold, waiting
At the bottom of my very deep sea
For the diver's light.

ASH WEDNESDAY RECKONING

Nueva Cadiz, city of pearls
Big as fists
On the isle of Cubagua
Now dust & ruin
In the blare of Caribbean sun —
Rifted margins of rubble tell much:
Slave trade,
Cathedral, painted saints.

Flora is meager, low-lying cactus,
Purple teasel, hill melons,
Poor man's friend —
Behind the village shacks on the shore,
Feral goats, lost hares.
The fisherman's sun-beaten & gnarled hand
Holds an open oyster
Squinting a too-small pearl
In this little hell.

Earthquake & age do their work.
Everything ends.
All of this oppresses. Newsprint darkens my fingers,
On my couch, silk-screened
Elephants in search of water & leaf
Reproach me —
Do they dream of being horses?

SORROW

A wet-winter rockslide crashes down,
Smashes asphalt.

Stuck in a car unable to move,
Light rain falling,

I will a cataphract of studded armor
To ward off

The long winding reach of the irrevocable,
Loss of arm or vision

Or heart.

I wish it were a year from now,
This boulder

Shrunk to a pebble
I shift from one pocket to another,

Trying never
To put it in my mouth.

ALL HORSES DIE

Lazarus pony staked to graze
Mowing to the mournful circumference
Of ever-returning home,

My father on his tractor
Moving earth around, mother fearful
On the impossible lawn —

Lumber pile & rusty nail, old
Ice box, fallen
Live oak limb — I am all

Made of glass, & so
Might break
Into shivering fragments,

No head, no eyes, no hair,
A ghost in the directions
Back — swift & I am there.

SENTIMENTAL EDUCATION

A pet goat died eating poisoned roses,
My mother told me he was just sleeping.

A pony died of colic, even though
We walked him through the night.

Each spring a calf was slaughtered,
The meat frozen, its name forgotten.

Death was a kind of earth I walked on,
Rolled in, dug up, tasted.

I rode in mountains I thought were human,
Chewing my hair & the leather reins.

I watched a crescent cut on my finger heal
& dreamed of having a baby.

JULIET'S LAMENT

I am lost in your absence,
Head turned toward Erebus,
Mouth of ash,
Handful of half-burned heart,
Mine.

Breath comes short
Standing in the stone stairway
Up from the tunnel,
Past hope, past cure, past help,
The brewery & the old stable
Snowed on, beaten by rain,
Flowered & hallowed.

If I could, I'd kill every wind,
Every wakened warrior at birth.

Every battle-drawn sword would melt
In me, iron-soled, cold,
Invincible —

School Clothes

Fabric raced under the speeding
Needle of her horse-shaped machine,
Dresses flew from the streaking silver,
Floated like ribbons
In the north wind of fairy tales.

I learned the mysteries of threading,
Snaked a strand through the horse's ears,
Down to the nostrils, into a sliver of light,
Sliding open the metal door to the pit
Where the bobbin whirred.

She looks up & asks, "Am I still alive?"
Her dead hands, just like mine.

NORTH WOOD

Not one breath drawn,
Perfectly formed
Small mistake in nature, still-
Birth in the field,
From the distance, a piece of tire
Or a saddle left out.

The budding trees up-pasture
Feel heavy.
There should be a colt here,
Life, motion,
A struggling to stand.

That night I tell my daughter
Who is sometimes afraid
Of the dark, "The black horse
Must survive winter."
Though she is a city girl, she sees
How true it is.

THE CALM AT THE END OF THE WORLD

Is ice. I look for you here though I know
You have died, summer's outrider, your

Spattered boots & sweaty sheep's wool
Are packed away in a deep drawer

Now. The tin siding of your house
Needs paint. I labor in the nerve bank,

Remembering rough grasses & heather,
Counting, cold sliding in

Behind my eyes, a season of glaciers,
An unfathered land.

You ride over hardened ash, black
Lava from the year I was born,

Leading horses in a sinuous line,
Tails like flames.

The Origin of Salt

The almighty rush of whirlpool
In Pentland Firth
Scares the hubris out of sailors,
Drags ships under.
They say there is a giant mill
At the bottom
Turned by a green-eyed witch,
Hands cut off
& tongue, eyes pinned open,
Grinding
Everything swallowed. Everything.

I have learned three things in the north:
The sea has a lung,
The dead do not eat grass, nor
Do they return.

FAIRY QUEEN

The glamour is not entirely working,
Sticks of straw beneath my gown,
Hag lines spider out from the corners
Of my extravagantly painted eyes,
Still, I have courage.

The poet & I have differences,
She says her religion is velvet,
I say my mother was a horse,
It's the difference between covering the body
Beautifully & being the body,
Mute & sweaty
In the long last heave of homestretch.

Still, the pen finds its way to my hand,
The white page fills with the runes of my story,
"The Girl with No Mother,"
How does it go?

Bread Loaf and the Bakeless Prizes

The Katharine Bakeless Nason Literary Publication Prizes were established in 1995 to expand the Bread Loaf Writers' Conference's commitment to the support of emerging writers. Endowed by the LZ Francis Foundation, the prizes commemorate Middlebury College patron Katharine Bakeless Nason and launch the publication career of a poet, a fiction writer, and a creative nonfiction writer annually. Winning manuscripts are chosen in an open national competition by a distinguished judge in each genre. Winners are published by Graywolf Press.

2011 Judges

Carl Phillips
Poetry

Stacey D'Erasmo
Fiction

Lynn Freed
Creative Nonfiction

Jo Sarzotti is the author of *Mother Desert,* winner of the Katharine Bakeless Nason Prize for Poetry, selected by Carl Phillips and awarded by Middlebury College and the Bread Loaf Writers' Conference. Her poetry has appeared in *Alaska Quarterly Review, Denver Quarterly,* and *North American Review,* among other publications. She lives in New York City and is Professor of Literature and director of Liberal Arts at The Juilliard School.

Book design by Connie Kuhnz. Composition by BookMobile Design and Publishing Services, Minneapolis, Minnesota. Manufactured by Versa Press on acid-free, 30 percent postconsumer wastepaper.